To Mark-Paul:

Hope you find a ray
of sunshine
in that icy heaven.

• • • • • • • • • • •

D1455432

CONTENTS

SATURDAY'S
STAR

His smile is innocent. But the glimmer in his hazel eyes suggests a trick or two. Are you willing to go along with it?

The challenge in Mark-Paul's eyes is clear. It's the look of a young actor determined to perform, destined to succeed at anything he chooses. He hates to be called a star. But it's the only way to describe Mark-Paul Gosselaar, the golden boy of NBC's hit show "Saved by the Bell."

For viewers across America, Saturday mornings have not been the same since "Saved by the Bell" first aired in 1989. With a cast of six dynamic teenagers, and Mark-Paul in the lead, it's the only live-action show on TV that kids can call their own.

But the colorful, wacky show also started a romantic phenomenon among Saturday morning viewers. "Saved by the Bell" brought Mark-Paul into the homes—and the hearts—of kids. Since then, his popularity has spread like a flash fire.

In his role as Zack Morris, one of the coolest guys at Bayside High, Mark-Paul captures the admiration of kids everywhere. No one can resist Zack's antics as he schemes to win a bet, save the school, or get a date with the girl of his dreams. His pranks usually get him into some tricky spots along the way. But with a little quick thinking and fast talking, Zack finds his way out of trouble— guaranteeing a barrel of laughs.

For Zack, the halls of Bayside High School are paved with opportunities for fun. And from the sound of the cheering fans in the audience at each taping of "Saved by the Bell," the Hollywood boulevards are paved with golden opportunities for Mark-Paul Gosselaar.

People magazine dubbed Mark-Paul "the latest heir to the Great Teen Throb mantle once worn by Kirk Cameron and Corey Haim." *Splice* magazine has called him "one of daytime's brightest stars." And he's been touted as the guy "who lights up TV screens" by the popular teen publication *Dream Guys*.

It takes a talented actor to bring a character like Zack to life. But Mark-Paul insists that he's very different from the outgoing prankster he plays. "I'm much more shy," he says. Mark-Paul adds that he's not quite as smooth as the legendary Zack Morris. While Zack is a bit of a con man, Mark-Paul believes in playing it straight, especially with girls and friends.

His costars agree. "Mark-Paul and Zack? They're total opposites," says Tiffani-Amber Thiessen, the dark-haired beauty who plays Kelly Kapowski on "Saved by the Bell." "Zack's a preppy. He always looks for the easy way out. Mark-Paul's a lot more active, into sports."

"Mark-Paul's kind of shy," says Lark Voorhies, the young actress who plays Lisa Turtle, the fashion queen of the show. Lark points out that Mark-Paul often keeps to himself on the set by finding a quiet, off-to-the-side place to sit during rehearsals.

Since Mark-Paul is in almost every scene of "Saved by the Bell," he can't wander off too far.

And when it comes time to tape the show on Fridays, Mark-Paul's performance is crucial. Between takes on the set, he stands by patiently and waits for instructions from the director. But the moment the director calls for another take, Mark-Paul's face comes alive.

As Tom Tenowich, supervising producer, puts it, Mark-Paul is "sort of a shy, quiet guy. But when we tape on Fridays, he kicks into another gear."

The stage manager calls out, "In five . . . four . . . three . . . two . . ." And like a flash of lightning, there's electricity on the set. The confident grin on Mark-Paul's handsome face tells us that he's in character. Energy is high. Zack is back.

And the audience loves it. Between takes, a cheerleading squad visiting from northern

California scrambles down to the stage floor and shouts out a cheer for the cast of the show. A middle-school choir sings a slow version of "Happy Birthday" for Mark-Paul in four-part harmony.

Then, on the count of three, a group of excited fans in the back row of the studio audience call out, "We love you, Mark-Paul!"

Shielding his eyes against the lights, Mark-Paul peers up at the well-wishers. He smiles and salutes them with a wave of his hand. Despite the heat of the lights and the pressure of performing, he finds a moment to greet his fans.

What drives this actor who's winning hearts around the world?

There's more to Mark-Paul Gosselaar than a handsome face and a warm smile. You may have watched him spend the first half of his teen years on Saturday-morning television. But to discover the real Mark-Paul, you need to step behind the scenes.

JUST
A NORMAL
KID

Mark-Paul Gosselaar was born on March 1, 1974, in Panorama City, a town in the San Fernando Valley. He was the fourth child born to Paula and Hans Gosselaar, Dutch immigrants who brought their family to America in March 1966. Mark-Paul has an older brother named Mike, and two older sisters: Sylvia and Linda.

Dark eyed and petite, his mother, Paula Gosselaar, explains the family's unique history: "I was raised half in Indonesia and half in Holland," Paula says. Her father, Mark-Paul's maternal grandfather, worked for the Shell Corporation in Indonesia.

Paula first met Mark-Paul's father, Hans, when they were both young kids growing up in a Dutch community in Indonesia. "We went to school together, and he was always in the neighborhood playing ball," Paula says of Hans. But there was no real romance in those early years—just friendship.

The sudden death of Paula's father prompted her family to move back to Holland. But as fate would have it, she saw Hans again. The political events of World War II caused his family also to return to the Netherlands.

"It happened that his friends were living close by, and we met again," Paula explains. From her point of view, there was only one snag in the romance. "He liked my sister, and I liked him," she says with a grin.

Determined to catch his eye, Paula would stop by with her bicycle, trying to look "scuffed up" to win the heart of Hans, a bicycling enthusiast. "We would bike from The Hague to Brussels—very long treks," says Paula. "It was a lot of fun.

"Finally, my sister fell in love with someone else, and he thought, 'Oh, well, I'm going to take this little one.' After awhile—I don't know—maybe he liked me," she says with a chuckle. She adds, "Though we didn't get married on the bike."

In March 1966 the Gosselaars decided to move their three children to the United States. They were eager to join the relatives who had already settled in California, and they couldn't resist the lure of America.

"When I went on vacation here, I loved the country," says Mark-Paul's mother. "I loved the people and the weather—maybe because I grew up in Indonesia and the climate is so similar here."

Hans Gosselaar found work as a supervisor in a manufacturing plant in California. Paula decided to remain a full-time mom. As a result of their upbringing, all the Gosselaar children speak fluent Dutch.

Eight years after the family arrived in California, Mark-Paul was born. His mother remembers Mark-Paul's childhood fondly. "He was a very easy child. I cannot say a wrong word about this boy. I wish I could, but . . . " Her words trail off with a mischievous laugh, much like her son's.

"Back when he was little, he was perfect," Paula says. "He was perfect in school. He was perfect at home. When I'd say, 'Mark-Paul, do this,' he did it."

According to Mark-Paul, his childhood was similar to the early years of most kids in America. "When I was little, I was just a normal, average kid. I was nothing special," he says with a shrug. He's almost apologetic. But Mark-Paul Gosselaar's typical childhood may be the solid basis that makes him such a healthy, well-rounded guy today.

Although Mark-Paul was the first Gosselaar child to be born in America, he wasn't the first to catch the attention of theatrical agents. When Mark-Paul's brother and sisters were kids, they turned many heads, too.

"My older children were approached many times," Mark-Paul's mother explains. "People approached me at the beach when the children were little. And one time, on an airplane, someone said, 'I'd like to use your daughter.'"

The person was a talent scout for a modeling agency. He begged Paula Gosselaar to sign her daughter up at the agency, but Paula never made it into the agent's office.

Instead, all the attention her children received made her nervous. "I thought, They look the same as other kids, so why do these people want *my* children?" Paula remembers with a laugh. "I was an immigrant and I was scared. I was not raised that way."

New to America, Mark-Paul's mother was not yet familiar with the classic Hollywood dream. Could it be true that, in this land of opportunity, ordinary people were discovered and turned into stars?

When Mark-Paul came along and people kept complimenting Paula on her younger son, she decided to give him a shot at modeling.

"It was more or less a friend's idea," Paula explains. This friend made an appointment for Mark-Paul at a talent agency. "I went to the agency with him, and that's how it all got started," says Paula.

More than ten years later, Mark-Paul still

remembers his first job. "The first thing I did was a print ad for Century Plaza. I was five." He smiles as he thinks back to those early days.

Although Mark-Paul was just a kindergartner when he got his first modeling assignment, he enjoyed the work. "At that time, when he was little, he liked it," says his mother.

Photographers captured that engaging Gosselaar grin and those shining eyes in snapshots taken for print ads. As a young boy, Mark-Paul was able to open magazines and see himself smiling back in a handful of advertisements.

"He loved modeling," says his mother. "And I have to say, he was very good. Everybody loved this little boy. And he loved it."

Still, no one knew the incredible talents that would eventually emerge from the wide-eyed boy with sandy blond hair. Eventually, Mark-Paul was the one who pushed his parents to let him try something else.

His mother remembers fielding Mark-

Paul's questions. "He started doing modeling," Paula recalls. "Then there came a time when he was asking questions: 'Why can't I do commercials?' And I said, 'Well, to do that, you have to learn something about acting.' So we put him in a workshop."

Although Mark-Paul's parents didn't steer him into show business, the Gosselaars tried to teach their son the importance of commitment. "I never pushed him into anything," Mark-Paul's mother explains.

But whatever field their son chooses to pursue, the Gosselaars want Mark-Paul to dedicate himself—100 percent. His mother adds, "I always told him, 'If you do something, you have to do the best you can and not take anything for granted.'"

What prompted Mark-Paul to take a shot at acting? He remembers the exact moment when the idea occurred to him. "It was *Annie,* the musical," says Mark-Paul. His hazel eyes glimmer as he thinks back to the day his mother took him to see the show in Los Angeles. "I saw the show and liked the idea that a kid got to play a part."

Mark-Paul is still a fan of the popular musical. On one of his days off, he recently attended a production of *Annie* in Pasadena, California.

And things really came full circle for him when he got a chance to meet the actress who played Annie in the production he saw so many years ago. "I told her that she inspired me to go into show business," he says, thrilled at the chance to talk with her. "It was really neat."

Although six-year-old Mark-Paul did well in his acting workshop, his mother didn't know what to expect when she took him to his first audition for a TV commercial. Paula remembers a moment of panic as she waited in the casting director's office. "I don't know how the other mothers felt, but I was terrified," she admits. Paula worried that Mark-Paul wouldn't follow the director's instructions. "I thought, Maybe he's not going to do what they ask him to do," she recalls, adding, "You never know with kids."

But Paula Gosselaar's fears were unfounded. Mark-Paul came through with flying colors, impressing the casting director and the client, and surprising his parents.

Over the years, Mark-Paul frequently beat out other child actors in auditions for TV commercials. He enjoyed the work, but it was not without its problems. At one point, it seemed as if a chocolate cookie was going to signal the end of his career!

It happened when Mark-Paul was taping a commercial for Oreo cookies. The director wanted him to toss a cookie in the air and catch it in his mouth. Easy as pie! Piece of cake!—or at least Mark-Paul thought so, until he gave it a try. And then another . . . and then another. After dozens of attempts, and dozens of broken cookies, Mark-Paul began to think it couldn't be done.

At last, after what seemed like a hundred tosses, he did it! Mark-Paul had beat the cookie challenge. What a relief!

For the Gosselaar family, Mark-Paul's role in the 1988 PBS television movie *Necessary Parties* marked a turning point in his career.

Since the film was shot in Westchester County, the production company flew thirteen-year-old Mark-Paul and his mother east to New York City.

With a note of pride, Mark-Paul recalls the experience of filming on location. He loved the chance to see a different part of the country. "We shot some scenes in White Plains," he explains, "and there was a court-room scene in Yonkers."

Mark-Paul also enjoyed the break from the frantic pace of Hollywood. "It was a lot more peaceful," he says.

Also starring Alan Arkin, *Necessary Parties* is about a teenager who sues his parents for getting divorced. Mark-Paul plays Chris Mills, the main character who, underneath his anger, wants to keep his family together.

The role was a challenge for Mark-Paul. It was also his first chance to sink his teeth into a meaty acting part. From the light in his eyes when he speaks of the experience, you can tell that Mark-Paul will never forget that role.

His performance in the film took many

people by surprise. Even his parents were awed by the powerful performance delivered by their youngest child. As his mother watched the filming, she began to realize the depth of Mark-Paul's talent.

"I was shocked," says Paula Gosselaar. "The way he acted, the way he took the whole show in control—it was amazing."

Now that the film is available on video, a wider audience will have a chance to catch Mark-Paul Gosselaar in a more serious role.

By the time Mark-Paul entered the teen years, he had some fairly impressive credits on his résumé. However, when the time came to audition for "Good Morning, Miss Bliss," Mark-Paul still got a case of audition jitters.

Produced for the Disney channel, the new show featured British actress Hayley Mills playing the schoolteacher Miss Bliss.

The first audition was routine. His agent sent him to try out for the show. With his usual burst of enthusiasm, Mark-Paul held up the script and read for the part of Zack before a roomful of casting directors, producers, and Disney executives.

Mark-Paul thought the reading went well. He was right. The casting director called him back for a second audition. Then Mark-Paul's hopes began to rise—along with his anxiety. The problem was, he was called back five times before the producer could tell him that he'd landed the part of Zack Morris.

Mark-Paul remembers those auditions vividly. "It was nerve-racking," he says. "It was between me and this other kid. I was left hanging the whole time." The intensity in his voice reveals some of the pressure he felt during those crucial readings.

Then his face breaks into a grin, and Mark-Paul chuckles. "I thought I was going to get it," he adds, sounding more like Zack than the low-key Mark-Paul. "But you never know."

Why so many callbacks?

"The casting was essential," says Peter Engel, executive producer. He had a clear idea of the type of actors needed to play all the parts, and the character of Zack required an actor with extraordinary talent. Peter adds, "There was only one Zack in the United States."

Peter Engel smiles when he considers the role of Zack. "He's the biggest schemer in the world," he says. "But Zack will always do the right thing when it comes down to it. He may scam all the way, but he will always tell the truth in the end." It was important to find an actor that could portray Zack as a crafty kid, but a likable guy, too. Mark-Paul had exactly what the executive producer was looking for.

At last, Mark-Paul got a phone call from Peter Engel himself. Despite all the pressures of putting together a new show, Peter took the time to call all the actors personally after the casting was completed. He told Mark-Paul that he had earned the role of the one and only Zack Morris.

From the very beginning of "Good Morning, Miss Bliss," Peter had high hopes for the future of Mark-Paul Gosselaar. "I thought Gosselaar was going to be a teen star," the executive producer says, "but we didn't know what we had."

No one knew that Mark-Paul Gosselaar had just been cast in a role that would turn his life inside out—and upside down!

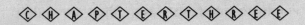
YOU'LL BE
SAVED BY
THE BELL

After its debut on the Disney channel, "Good Morning, Miss Bliss" experienced some growing pains that had nothing to do with its young cast members.

One big change was a move from Los Angeles to Florida. The actors and crew were asked to be prepared to pack up and travel across the country so that the show could be shot in Disney's new studios in Orlando, Florida.

The prospect of leaving Los Angeles did not thrill Mark-Paul and his parents. He didn't want to leave his friends behind. His father couldn't afford to leave his job. And his mother had just taken a part-time position as a ground hostess for an airline.

"I had just gotten my new job, and I didn't want to give that up," says Mark-Paul's mother. But she and Mark-Paul's father didn't want to stand in the way of their son's career. Although Mark-Paul was only fourteen at the time, his parents left the final decision up to him.

With a heavy heart, Mark-Paul went on his own to meet with the show's producers. But instead of having to make a difficult decision, he came away with some exciting news.

The deal with Disney was off, but NBC was interested in picking up the show with a new twist. There would be a whole new look, a new focus, a new name, and new cast members. But the character of Zack, as played by Mark-Paul Gosselaar, would figure prominently in the new show.

What was the exciting new twist? A show about kids, for kids, starring kids.

At the end of each school day, there's one sound heard across America that's pure music to kids' ears—the bell that signals the end of the school day. When you're on the spot in class, isn't it great to be saved by the bell?

This was part of the premise behind the original idea that executive producer Peter Engel had for a TV series. Instead of focusing on serious social crises, he wanted to produce a show that dealt with the everyday problems shared by teenagers around the world—problems like grades, peer pressure, and the rocky road to romance.

Peter's vision was shared by an executive at NBC. Brandon Tartikoff, then president of NBC Entertainment, liked Peter's plan to feature six kids who had been together since grade school. "Six kids coming of age, going through rites of passage . . . six kids who love each other and will always help each other," Peter recalls.

Using the story idea from "Good Morning, Miss Bliss," which he also produced, Peter Engel wrote the first script for "Saved by the Bell."

When the time came to choose the cast for

the show, Engel began a nationwide talent hunt. Although Mark-Paul Gosselaar, Lark Voorhies, and Dustin Diamond were picked up from the cast of "Miss Bliss," there were still three important spots to fill.

"We searched all over the country," says Peter. The producer viewed videotapes of child actors from New York, Miami, Chicago, Dallas, and Atlanta.

In the end, every actor chosen to play one of the six kids happened to live in southern California—except Elizabeth Berkley, who plays Jessie, the knockout with brains. She was visiting Los Angeles from her home state of Michigan. Mario Lopez, the streetwise Slater, lived just a few hours south in San Diego. Tiffani-Amber Thiessen, the show's beauty, lived an hour or so from Los Angeles in Long Beach, California.

Even the actor chosen to play Mr. Belding, the principal, was working in theater in nearby Santa Monica. Dennis Haskins, the talented actor who's always putting the finger on Zack, was appearing onstage in a musical. The producers of "Saved by the Bell" came to the show to see another actress, and ended up coming away with the man in charge of Bayside High.

And, amazingly, the "only Zack in the United States," Mark-Paul Gosselaar, was living right on the outskirts of Los Angeles.

Mark-Paul worked on those first few episodes of "Saved by the Bell" with his usual electric enthusiasm. But the atmosphere on the set was tentative. There was no guarantee that the show would be a success.

As Peter Engel puts it, "We believed in our concept. The big question was, would it work on the screen?"

The answer?

"Well, after one show," Engel says, snapping his fingers, "it was there." The chemistry between the actors was just right.

But when the show aired on prime time, it received mixed reviews. Big-city TV critics panned the show. It was as if "Saved by the Bell" were being penalized for being too wholesome, too in tune with the concerns of normal kids.

Looking back on that time, Engel shakes

his head. "I'm just so proud of these kids," he says. "They didn't stand a chance. This whole thing didn't stand a chance of ever succeeding. We had only one person who thought it could succeed, and that was Brandon."

Fortunately, Brandon Tartikoff stood behind the show. His support gave "Saved by the Bell" a chance to succeed against all odds.

Despite the critics' barbs, Peter wanted to go on. "Their criticism fueled me more to say, 'I'm going to believe in the kids of America, in the kids of this country. I believe this show is for them, and they will be there in the audience.'" He sits back and folds his arms. "And they were."

In what Peter calls "a bold, new approach," NBC decided to air the show on Saturday mornings, pitting it against cartoons.

Saturday-morning TV was an exclusive cartoon kingdom. You just had to turn on your set to see the world through animation. Colorful creatures bounce through polka-dotted meadows. Flashy superheroes, straight out of comic books, save the city. And talking animals chase each other through the house while the people are away.

Could a sitcom compete with cartoons?

The Saturday-morning placement of "Saved by the Bell" was considered risky when the show first premiered in the fall of 1989. But the sitcom attracted an audience, and that audience steadily grew until "Saved by the Bell" became the top-rated Saturday-morning show among teens.

Mark-Paul didn't need to see the ratings to know that kids were watching the show. He had a taste of the show's success just after it premiered. "Saved by the Bell" had only been on the air for a few weeks when young girls began mobbing the NBC studios where the show is taped.

Peter Engel remembers getting a phone call from NBC security. He was still at work in his office in the studio when the mob of fans assembled. "They called me from the lobby and said: 'The kids won't leave!' " The group of fans wanted to catch a glimpse of Mark-Paul Gosselaar before they would go home.

By the time Peter reached the lobby, Mark-Paul was standing in the corridor, waiting to go out and greet the girls. Engel recalls the moment when Mark-Paul turned to him and said, "Please, walk with me." When the producer agreed to go with him, Mark-Paul added, "Don't leave me alone." The crowd of screaming females was enough to frighten anyone.

The mob of girls was overwhelming for a fourteen-year-old kid who'd never even been asked for an autograph. But Peter and the NBC executives were delighted. Rarely did a show get such a positive reaction so soon after its debut.

Just before Mark-Paul and his producer faced the crowd, Peter Engel remembers turning to Mark-Paul's mother and saying: "Mark-Paul Gosselaar is going to be a star— if we do our job right."

A WEEK
IN THE
LIFE . . .

When we imagine the lives of our favorite stars, we think of bright lights, limousines, and outrageous parties.

Few people outside the acting arena realize how demanding an actor's schedule can be. Here's your chance to follow Mark-Paul Gosselaar during a normal week of taping "Saved by the Bell."

Monday
6:30 A.M.

Mark-Paul pulls himself out of bed and ducks into the shower. Then he grabs a quick breakfast and heads out the door.

7:00 A.M.

Mark-Paul and his mom jump into the car for the drive to the NBC studios in Burbank. It'll take at least forty minutes on the freeway—and with L.A. traffic, you have to give yourself some extra time.

8:00 A.M.

Time for school! Mark-Paul reports to the classroom on the set, where he has his own desk. Monday is an especially heavy school day for Mark-Paul. Today a teacher from the Learning Post, his high school, visits the set to test Mark-Paul and make sure he's keeping up with his assignments.

NOON

After four hours of algebra, science, and English in the studio classroom, Mark-Paul heads to the stage for the table reading. He and the other cast members actually sit around the table and read the script aloud for the first time. This gives the writers a chance to see which lines are funny, and which scenes could use a little sprucing up.

1:00 P.M.

Lunchtime—at last! Mark-Paul heads off to a nearby Thai restaurant to grab a bite with Tiffani and Mario.

2:00 P.M.

Mark-Paul is back in the studio for rehearsal. Today the director "blocks" the scenes, which means he shows the actors how to move through each scene, where to stand on the set, and what doors to use for entrances and exits. The actors are still reading from their scripts.

5:30 P.M.

It's quitting time! Mark-Paul and his mother drive home. After dinner, there's just enough time for a quick game of Nintendo. Then Mark-Paul hits those schoolbooks and does some homework.

Tuesday

6:30 A.M.

Is it that time already? With a yawn, Mark-Paul gets up and gets ready for work.

8:00 A.M.

Zack may be saved by the bell, but Mark-Paul has to report to the classroom on the set and crack open his textbooks.

NOON

Mark-Paul reports to the stage for rehearsal. He has a brand-new script that was slipped under his dressing room door by one of the production assistants. The writers have changed a few lines after hearing how the script sounded in yesterday's table reading.

1:00 P.M.

Lunchtime! Mark-Paul grabs a sandwich he brought from home, finds a sunny spot on the studio lot, and soaks up some rays.

2:00 P.M.

It's back to rehearsal.

4:30 P.M.

The studio is now crowded with people at the fringes of the set. It's time for the network and producers' run-through. Mark-Paul and the other actors perform the entire show (though it's still a little rough) for NBC executives; Tom Tenowich, supervising producer; producers Peter Engel and Franco

Bario; and the writers. This gives the network a chance to suggest last-minute changes. The writers and producers also watch for any scenes or lines that need to be revised.

5:30 P.M.

After the run-through, Mark-Paul heads home for dinner, a game of basketball with his buddy from across the street, and some homework.

Wednesday

6:30 A.M.

Would someone please turn off that alarm clock?

8:00 A.M.

Mark-Paul is back in school on the set. Although he's already fluent in Dutch, today he's studying French, the language of *l'amour*.

NOON

It's back to the set for an hour of rehearsal. Today Mark-Paul received the third version of the script with more changes. This is the script that will be used for Friday's taping, so it's time to buckle down and learn those lines.

1:00 P.M.

Food, glorious food!

2:00 P.M.

Mark-Paul reports to the set for rehearsal.

4:30 P.M.

Time for the producers' run-through. Mark-Paul and the cast perform the show from top to bottom so that the producers can see how it's coming along.

5:30 P.M.

Mark-Paul reports to wardrobe, where Elizabeth Bass, the show's costume designer, shows him the clothes he'll be wearing in this week's episode. He's got to try everything on. If there's a shirt or a pair of slacks that isn't right, Elizabeth needs to know so she can come up with another costume fast!

6:30 P.M.

Mark-Paul heads home. After dinner, he tackles his revised script and memorizes those lines, once and for all.

Thursday

6:30 A.M.

Yeeeooowzza! What's that noise?

8:00 A.M.

Today's school hour is just that—one hour. There's just enough time for a history lesson. Do you know who lives at Lincoln's Gettysburg address?

9:00 A.M.

Mark-Paul reports to the stage for today's rehearsal, which is called camera blocking. For the first time, the camera and sound crew are on the set, wheeling around huge cameras—four of them—and microphones called booms. In today's rehearsal, Mark-Paul doesn't need to "perform," but he has to pay attention to where the director wants him to stand. Otherwise, he might end up off-camera—and off your TV screen!

1:00 P.M.

Break for lunch. On days like this, Mark-Paul is tempted to eat anything that doesn't bite back!

2:00 P.M.

Mark-Paul reports back to the set to finish camera blocking. He can't be late! With thousands of dollars' worth of camera and sound equipment and dozens of people waiting, every minute means big money for the show's budget.

4:30 P.M.

Mark-Paul rushes backstage and ducks into a "quick-change" room—a cubicle that looks a lot like a dressing room at your local department store. He changes into his costume for the opening scene of this week's show.

4:45 P.M.

Onstage once again, Mark-Paul waits for the director to cue the opening scene for a full tech run-through. He and the cast will perform the show from beginning to end, this time with the cameras in place. This gives the director and producers a chance to make sure that the camera angles, costumes, and lighting are just right.

6:30 P.M.

After the run-through, Mark-Paul changes out of his costume and heads home. He needs to keep a low profile on Thursday nights. Tomorrow is the big day!

Friday

7:00 A.M.

Hurray for an extra half hour of sleep! Mark-Paul springs out of bed at the sound of the alarm. It's taping day—time to put together everything that he's been rehearsing and practicing all week.

8:30 A.M.

Mark-Paul reports to the on-set classroom for one hour of school. He hurries to finish an algebra equation before the time is up.

9:30 A.M.

Back in his dressing room, Mark-Paul quickly changes into his costume for the first scene of the show.

9:40 A.M.

Makeup? Yes, even the guys on "Saved by the Bell" have to wear it! Mark-Paul reports to a large room. The walls are covered with mirrors. There are two sinks, and the linoleum counters are covered with jars and trays of makeup. While Mark-Paul sits patiently in a chair, the makeup artist covers his face with a heavy foundation. All the actors on camera need makeup so that they don't look pale and washed out when they appear on your TV screen.

10:00 A.M.

The hairstylist gives Mark-Paul's sandy blond head a quick combing. Unlike other stars, Mark-Paul usually takes care of his own hair, which doesn't require any special treatment. No fuss, no muss!

10:30 A.M.

Mark-Paul is onstage, ready for the director's cue. This morning, Mark-Paul and the rest of the cast will perform the show in costume and makeup. The cameras tape everything. The show that you see on TV is usually the performance taped in the afternoon, before a live audience. But as a precaution, the producers keep the tape made during the morning. If there's a mishap during the afternoon taping, they can slip in a scene or two from the morning performance.

2:30 P.M.

The cast and crew of "Saved by the Bell" gather together for a very special dinner in a back room of the huge studio. There are tables laden with food—everything from vegetable lasagna to juicy roast beef. One table features delicious desserts—Oreo ice-cream cake, praline pie, and chocolate cheesecake. Time to fill up a plate and dig in! Everyone needs energy for the big show.

2:45 P.M.

While Mark-Paul and the other cast members eat, director Don Barnhart reads off the last-minute notes he's made on his script. Don goes through the show scene by scene, reminding the actors of special cues, warning them about problem areas, and pointing out lines that they need to deliver with more "punch." As the actors eat, they listen soberly, nodding when the director gives them a word of advice.

3:30 P.M.

Mark-Paul and the "Saved by the Bell" gang head back to the stage to prepare for the show. Once again, the actors have to change into their costumes for the opening scene.

3:40 P.M.

After changing his clothes, **Mark-Paul** visits the makeup room. All the actors need touch-ups before they can go on camera again.

3:50 P.M.

As Mark-Paul waits backstage, he can hear executive producer Peter Engel onstage, talking to the audience. Engel introduces some of the people who work on the show and then calls off the names of the actors. Mark-Paul can hear the audience applauding as his costars run out to the stage.

3:52 P.M.

Mark-Paul is the last one to be introduced. He steps out into the bright lights and waves at the audience. A roar of applause greets him. Some of the girls are screaming, and some of the guys in the audience yell out a cheer. Mark-Paul gets a charge out of the wild reception. What a thrill!

3:55 P.M.

Backstage, the actors gather in a tight huddle as their director gives them a quick pep talk. They listen carefully, then press close, their hands clasped in the center of the circle. "Yeah!" Mark-Paul shouts with the others as they promise to do their best. Then the cast scatters, and Mark-Paul hurries off to his position for the opening scene.

4:00 P.M.

The cameras are rolling for the final taping. This is the highlight of Mark-Paul's week. He's alive with energy and enthusiasm—and the audience can't help but respond. Each scene is greeted with a rush of laughter and a burst of applause. Although the entire show is taped on Friday morning, the version you see on the air is usually this one, with the live audience. The audience makes the "Saved by the Bell" actors come alive.

4:15 P.M.

As soon as the first scene ends, Mark-Paul runs backstage, where everyone is moving about frantically. The stage manager gives him a gentle shove into the quick-change room, which is the size of a medium-sized closet. Dustin Diamond is already inside, tugging on a shirt. There are separate quick-change rooms for the girls and guys. There's also a separate room for the guest stars. And it's a good thing. These rooms are so tiny, if you aren't careful, two people could step into one pair of pants!

5:05 P.M.

Mark-Paul turns to the camera and breaks into one of Zack's craftiest grins. The audience groans. They know Zack's up to his usual scheming tricks!

6:25 P.M.

The studio is filled with the roar of applause as the crowd cheers one last time. The final scene has been taped, and the audience is tickled with the show's outcome. Peter Engel brings the cast out for bows, and Mark-Paul runs onstage to say good-bye to a fabulous audience.

6:30 P.M.

That's it for this week's show! Mark-Paul returns to his dressing room to wash off that heavy makeup and change back into his own jeans and T-shirt.

7:00 P.M.

Picking up his copy of next week's script—which he'll read over the weekend—Mark-Paul saunters out to the parking lot and heads home.

What's in the works for the weekend? The possibilities are endless!

Zack and Kelly haven't been dating for very long, but Mark-Paul and Tiffani have been friends since the show began!

With a face like that, stardom is guaranteed!

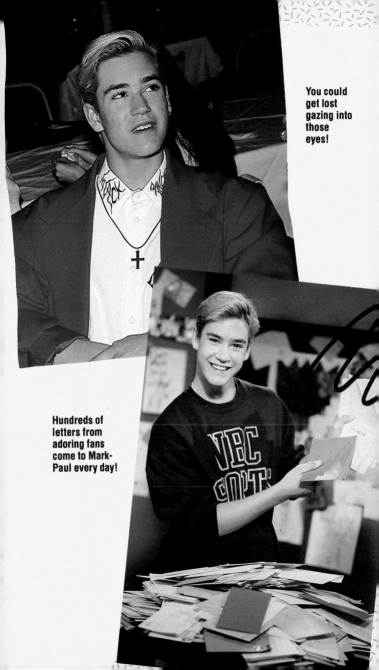

You could get lost gazing into those eyes!

Hundreds of letters from adoring fans come to Mark-Paul every day!

Another adorable Gosselaar! This one's his niece, Brittany-Paula.

The gang at the Max, the coolest hangout in Bayside!

Zack and Kelly—the
picture-perfect couple!

Behind
every
great star,
there's a
wonderful
Mom!

It takes
hard work
to make a
perfect show.

The work begins
as Mark-Paul and
Mario and the rest
of the cast sit
down to read
through the script
for the first time.

What scheme is Zack cooking up this week?

Even then, Mark-Paul was on the fast track!

CHAPTER FIVE

WONDERFUL
WEEKENDS

This week's show is a wrap. The red sun is setting over the rambling Hollywood Hills. For Mark-Paul Gosselaar, it's time to kick back and have some fun!

A total professional, Mark-Paul keeps his attention focused when he's working on the set of "Saved by the Bell." But when the workweek is over, as he puts it, "I go home—and that's when I really get loose."

When the show airs on Saturday mornings, Mark-Paul tries to watch himself on TV. He's eager to learn from his performance in past episodes. But Mark-Paul admits that he doesn't always catch the show. It's not easy for a guy who loves the outdoors to spend every Saturday morning at home!

Weekends are also the time to squeeze in an outing or two with a girl—but that's another story—and another chapter!

Just like any other teen in America, Mark-Paul spends a lot of his free time hanging out with his friends in the neighborhood. From swimming and biking to football and hoops, there's plenty to do in the pleasant suburban community the Gosselaars call home.

"My best friends aren't actors. They're guys from the neighborhood," says Mark-Paul. "I still know some of the people I went to kindergarten with."

Mark-Paul is often seen around the neighborhood with two of his best buddies, Nick and Derek. "We do crazy things—normal teenager things," Mark-Paul says with a shrug.

When the threesome is not shooting hoops or weight lifting at the local YMCA, they can be found recruiting other kids for an impromptu game of football. As far as Mark-Paul and his friends are concerned, the more the merrier. "We search the whole neighborhood and find anybody who wants to play," says Mark-Paul. "It doesn't matter who they are."

Most of all, Mark-Paul loves to get out in the sunshine and enjoy the outdoors. "I love the outdoors," he says with conviction. "The wind and the sun—it's great."

Did you expect something more exotic from this teen star?

Despite his celebrity status in Hollywood, at home, Mark-Paul insists that he's a regular guy. Although he earns a lot more than the average teen, his parents only let him spend a small portion of his salary—twenty dollars a week. The rest goes into a trust fund, which Mark-Paul plans to use for his college tuition.

But Mark-Paul's limited allowance doesn't keep him from doing the things he enjoys in his spare time. One of his most recent passions is dirt-bike racing. Though Mark-Paul himself doesn't race, he loves to watch his older brother, Mike, compete.

In this rigorous sport, bikers leap over man-made moguls and whip around sharp corners. Mud and sand go flying as the bike wheels spin wildly on the dirt track. Each event is exciting to watch, and Mark-Paul loves to cheer his brother on from the sidelines.

Besides enjoying neighborhood sports, Mark-Paul loves getting away to the ski slopes in the winter months. Having mastered downhill skiing, he recently took up snowboarding, which he describes as "skateboarding on the snow—with no wheels!"

In the summer months, Mark-Paul can be found on the beach with a boogie board or a body board. According to Mark-Paul, his idea of a dream vacation would be a chance to ride a body board in the Fiji Islands. For anyone whose geography is a little rusty, Fiji is a group of islands in the South Pacific, somewhere between Hawaii and New Zealand. Now, that's exotic!

But for today, the beach near Malibu will do just fine!

Mark-Paul has only been on a surfboard once. But he loves to catch a wave on a body board, which is a lighter board, made of Styrofoam instead of fiberglass.

A true Californian, Mark-Paul is hip to the unspoken etiquette of riding the waves. He's learned how to avoid aquatic blunders, which are considered "real uncool," says Mark-Paul.

"Like if someone cuts you off in the water and takes your line—that's uncool," he explains. "Whoever paddles out first gets the wave. Also, if you're paddling out, you try to get over the wave first, before the guy out there comes riding in."

So the next time you're walking on the beach and you see a tan, golden-haired hunk slicing through the water on a body board, you'd better look twice. It might be Mark-Paul Gosselaar catching a wave!

WE ARE
FAMILY

If executive producer Peter Engel could have sent out invitations to the cast and crew before the first taping of "Saved by the Bell," his message might have sounded something like this:

You are cordially invited to join the "Saved by the Bell" family. The hours are long, but the work is fun. Dress casual. Bring your own sense of humor. We'll supply the laughter. And please, leave your ego at the door.

In fact, the cast and crew of the show *do* get together for a party at the beginning and end of each season. And the producer has entertained everyone at his house a few times. "The kids come and swim and play paddle tennis and basketball," says Peter. They've even had a barbecue in the Engels' backyard.

These informal get-togethers give the young actors and crew a chance to celebrate the feeling that began in the first week of taping—the feeling of being a family.

"The family aspect is what makes it work," says Peter. Although Mark-Paul has a bigger role than any of the other cast members, he respects his co-workers. He knows the importance of being a team player.

Over the years, Mark-Paul has become good friends with his costars. He once met Lark at a ski resort where they spent some time on the slopes together. And the teen actors used to go out together every Friday night—despite the fact that they live in various parts of Los Angeles.

Watching the cast work and play together, you are reminded of the teasing, the rivalry, and the love among brothers and sisters.

"We've had our differences at times," admits Tiffani, "but we all get along really well now."

"We get along great!" Mario announces.

Mark-Paul sits back for a moment, listening to them. "A couple of times I've heard Mario say, 'I'm never going to talk to her again!' " he teases, nodding at Tiffani.

Everyone laughs as Mario denies it.

"Hey," Mario insists, "I don't know what *he's* talking about, but—"

"Ahh, Mario, come on!" Tiffani says, nudging him with her elbow.

Their jibing is all in good fun. But the truth of the matter is that the cast members of "Saved by the Bell" have had their differences over the years. When six teenagers work, play, and eat together nearly every day of the week, there's bound to be a little friction.

"We're together every day. It's almost like living together," Tiffani points out.

"I see more of them than I do my own sister," says Mario.

Elizabeth agrees. "I see more of them in a year than I see my parents and brother."

Lark admits, "We fight and we make up all the time."

"Then we fight again the next day," Dustin adds with a grin.

Peter Engel has helped the actors through a few rocky periods. "I remember one night when I had to sit with them for two hours over crushes—unrequited and unfulfilled—and cliques among six kids," he says.

Because the teens spend so much time together on the set, they don't have the luxury of hiding or just avoiding each other. Instead, they have to work out their differences.

Peter adds, "There were hard feelings, and we had to really talk it out. The 'family' was having a problem. But in this family, you can't ignore anyone because you're right here and self-contained."

Director Don Barnhart spends most of his waking hours with the teen actors. Watching him work with Mark-Paul and the other teenagers, you can see that Don loves and respects each and every one of them. Over the years, he has worked through various problems with the cast members.

Don recalls one occasion when he could tell that something was bothering Lark, the bright actress who plays Lisa. He took a moment to stop the rehearsal and sit down for a talk with her.

"I was so pained for her feelings," says Don. "Things came out of me that I never thought would come out. We sat there and cried together and held hands, and then hugged and went on about our business."

As director of the show, Don must maintain control while giving the actors the freedom they need to be creative—and just to be kids sometimes.

An energetic, patient man, Don is sensitive to the fact that his actors are human. "They have their troubles," he admits. "They will come to me on occasion, or they'll come to Peter. There are times on the set when you become the father figure or the authority figure."

At times, the director's authority seems ominous. In the second part of the week, Don sits in a special booth to view the show on TV monitors—through the eye of the camera. While he's in the booth, Don can only speak to the actors over a loudspeaker, which broadcasts his voice throughout the studio.

When there's a serious problem on the set, Don leaves the booth and comes out to talk to the actors personally. Since they try so hard to do each scene right, the actors dread the sight of their director marching out to correct them.

As Don walks out of the booth, the assistant director warns the actors over the loudspeaker: "He's coming out!"

Don smiles when he discusses the routine. "You come out of the booth on a tear and I hear them say: 'He's coming out!' Everybody gets real quiet."

Although he's never stern, Don needs to keep Mark-Paul and the other actors focused on the task at hand. "If you lose that control, then you've lost the show."

When working with Don, Mark-Paul is a supreme professional. With a serious frown, he listens intently whenever Don gives him pointers. Mark-Paul respects the director, but he's not afraid to ask questions when he doesn't understand Don's instructions.

Not every moment on the set is serious, though. The director points out, "On occasion, they start to giggle . . . and giggle. And you can't stop them."

The good-natured romping and laughter on the set give "Saved by the Bell" a special feeling. In the end, the fun, joyful spirit that comes through to viewers across America is the real thing.

While the teen actors have grown close, a bond also has formed between their real-life parents, who spend a lot of time on the set.

Peter Engel includes them in the "Saved by the Bell" family. "We've been blessed with six great kids—and six sets of parents who have worked with us," he says.

The actors' parents love the atmosphere on the set. As Tiffani's mom, Robin Thiessen, explains: "It's very family oriented. I don't think that any one of the kids feel that they can't go to one of the other kids with a teen problem."

By law, when the actors were under seventeen, they had to have one parent present on the set at all times. Since none of the kids had reached that age when taping first started, their parents got to see a lot of each other. The mothers became fast friends. Now they make it a point to spend time together.

"Anytime there's a function, we parents go so that we can see one another," says Tiffani's mother. "Whether it be Magic Mountain [at Disneyland], or at the beach, or skiing, or whatever."

Mark-Paul's mother went on a whirlwind trip to Mexico with Mario's mother, Elvia Lopez. Paula Gosselaar also goes shopping once a week with Tiffani's mom. Both women laugh about their comical experiences and dealing with traffic in Los Angeles.

"We're a close-knit group," Mark-Paul's mother explains. "We are fortunate."

When asked about the cast's close relationships, Mark-Paul and the rest usually joke about it.

When someone suggests that they're like brothers and sisters, Mario responds with a deadpan expression much like Slater's: "Well, I wouldn't get carried away."

"What does that make me?" asks Dennis, who plays the school principal. "Your uncle?"

"Grandfather!" Mario jibes.

"Grandfather Dennis!" Lark and Tiffani chant in unison.

Dennis throws up his arms in mock alarm. Although he's no longer a teenager, he's not that close to the golden years.

"Dennis is another one of our brothers," says Mark-Paul.

The rest of the cast agrees.

"He's the big brother," Tiffani says, her blue eyes flashing with appreciation.

The close bond between cast members is no accident. Peter Engel recalls, "From the first day, we said it had to be a family. Otherwise, we wouldn't make it."

From the laughter heard in the studio where "Saved by the Bell" is taped each week, it's obvious that Peter's philosophy works. This is one family that's going to stick together.

NO PLACE LIKE
HOME

It's not a palace or a mansion. Not an elaborate house with fancy gardens and sparkling fountains. Instead, the Gosselaar home is an attractive one-story house on top of a hill.

Partially hidden by fragrant rosebushes, the three-bedroom house seems modest for a star like Mark-Paul. Still, he feels very much at home in this suburban community forty minutes northwest of Los Angeles.

Since Mark-Paul's mother is still employed by an international airline, the Gosselaars take advantage of the perks and travel as often as they can. A seasoned traveler, Mark-Paul has visited Spain, France, England, and of course, Holland, where his father's relatives still live.

Mark-Paul's hazel eyes sparkle when he talks about venturing to new places and experiencing different cultures. He's a true explorer at heart. But when vacation time is over, there's no place like home.

During his childhood, Mark-Paul's family moved three times. Each time, they ventured farther into the San Fernando Valley, farther away from the frenetic activity of Los Angeles's fast lane.

"I never lived in Hollywood, never lived in Los Angeles," says Mark-Paul. "I've always lived outside the city. And as the city started spreading, we kept moving farther out."

When he's inside, Mark-Paul can be found in his room, stretched out over the patchwork quilt on his bed. It's the perfect place to study or to memorize lines from a script.

But most of the time, Mark-Paul tries to get out in the fresh air. With a turquoise pool and colorful roses, the Gosselaars' yard is a great place to relax. Mark-Paul enjoys swimming laps or just splashing around in the pool.

Besides his parents, Mark-Paul shares the house with his sister Sylvia, his toddling niece, Britney-Paula, who's just about to turn two, and a host of animals. The Gosselaars have five dogs, four cats, and two turtles—quite a menagerie for one family!

The turtles—Roger and Virginia—live in Mark-Paul's bedroom. The turtles belong to Mark-Paul, but he says that his favorite of all the family pets is the Chihuahua named Coco. Abused as a pup, Coco came to the Gosselaars through the help of a veterinarian friend.

While "Saved by the Bell" was on break, Mark-Paul befriended the tiny pup. But after he went back to work on the set, Coco missed him. "When I went to work and didn't see her much, she started not liking me," he says regretfully. Since then, Coco has gotten used to Mark-Paul's rigorous schedule. But Mark-Paul admits that most of the dogs pay more attention to his mother, "because my mom's real good with dogs."

Although the Gosselaars bought Coco, all

the other dogs were either gifts or strays who ended up on Mark-Paul's doorstep.

"Before Coco, we'd never bought a dog," says Mark-Paul. "The pit bull came to our door with a litter of puppies. The dalmatian is from another litter we raised. The dalmatian's mother was abused, so my mom took her in and she had thirteen little puppies. We had about twenty dogs at one time!"

The dogs and cats in the Gosselaar household get along very well, although the dogs sometimes fight among themselves. "The dalmatian attacks the poodle sometimes," says Mark-Paul. "Mostly because the poodle is so old—about nineteen years old."

Mark-Paul defends his pit bull adamantly. "Pit bulls aren't vicious," he says. "It's all the owners. You could hit them—you could do anything, and still they're very, very loyal dogs. I think they're the most loyal dogs out there."

Although Mark-Paul's busy schedule keeps him out of the house most of the time, when he returns home, the family pets greet him at the door. "I like animals," he admits.

"And animals and kids like me. They always come to me."

Judging by the way his young niece clings to his legs and giggles when he smiles, it's obvious that kids respond well to Mark-Paul. One day when Britney-Paula was visiting the set of "Saved by the Bell," she made a game of following Mark-Paul wherever he went—into the makeup room, into the classroom, down the hall to his dressing room. The minute he sat down, she climbed onto his lap and picked up one of his schoolbooks.

As she leafed through the book, Mark-Paul noticed a barrette slipping out of her hair. He took it out, smoothed back Britney-Paula's sandy brown hair, and clipped it in again. "Ouch!" she said. But a moment later, all was forgotten, and she snuggled back into his arms, holding the book up to her nose.

Seeing them together, the family resemblance is obvious. Britney-Paula has those wide, bright Gosselaar eyes and that mischievous grin.

As an uncle, Mark-Paul is attentive and gentle, although he doesn't make a fuss over his young nephews and niece. Since Mark-Paul's brother, Mike, has four sons, and his sister Linda has one son, there are quite a few kids to entertain when the family gets together. Mark-Paul's niece and nephews range in age from one and a half to nine.

At times, Mark-Paul feels a bit sorry for Britney-Paula, the only girl in the group. "It's five boys, one girl." He repeats, "Five boys, *one girl*. Every time she goes over to visit them, they're always picking on her. It's pretty funny."

The "little ones," Mark-Paul's niece and nephews, don't think it's at all unusual to tune in on Saturday morning and watch their uncle on TV.

And though Mark-Paul's siblings are proud of their brother's achievements, his star status doesn't earn him special treatment at home. When he helps Mike repair dirt bikes, Mark-Paul gets as greasy and grimy as any other mechanic in the field. And Mike makes sure that Mark-Paul pitches in when it comes to one of the most tedious parts of a mechanic's job—the cleanup.

Mark-Paul appreciates having a family that avoids the glitter of Hollywood and clings to old-fashioned values. "My mom never pushed me to be a star," says Mark-Paul, "though I hate that word. But she never pushed me to be 'Hollywood.' That's why we live so far away—to get away from it all."

Since it touches their lives, the Gosselaars approach show business as they would any other profession. Mike works as a grip on various TV shows. (Grips are responsible for moving heavy equipment and scenery.) Mark-Paul's sister Sylvia recently agreed to run his fan club. With hundreds of letters coming in every month, Mark-Paul needs Sylvia's help so that he can make sure every piece of fan mail is answered.

And as far as Mark-Paul's parents are concerned, star status means nothing when you break the rules at home. Although Zack often gets away with his pranks, if Mark-

Paul stays out too late or lets his grades slip, "he gets grounded like normal kids," says Paula Gosselaar.

But unlike Zack, Mark-Paul tries to stay out of trouble. "I could never do the things Zack does," says Mark-Paul. Mark-Paul wouldn't try to flood the school bathrooms, rig a school election, or trick a girl into liking him, as Zack has been known to do.

Instead, Mark-Paul's worst offense seems to be breaking curfew or playing too much Nintendo—just like thousands of other teenagers across America. Some things are truly universal.

CHAPTER EIGHT

GIRLS, GIRLS, **GIRLS!**

In every interview and in every personal appearance, there's one question that Mark-Paul can always count on: "Do you have a girlfriend?" ask fans and reporters.

Fortunately for the females of America, the answer to that one is a most definitive no.

The truth is, Mark-Paul adores—and re-spects—girls. He winds up on a date almost every weekend. But at this point in his life, he's decided that it's best not to tie himself down to one girl. He doesn't have the time to get involved in a serious relationship. And maybe he just hasn't met the right girl yet.

"I like dating different girls," Mark-Paul admits. "I stick with one for a weekend and check it out. Then I might spend the next weekend with someone else."

His costar, Tiffani-Amber Thiessen, enjoys teasing Mark-Paul about his love life. She tries to get a full report each Monday morning when they begin rehearsing a new episode.

Tiffani's blue eyes twinkle as she tells all. "He'll say: 'I had so much fun with this girl.' Then, after the next weekend he'll say: 'I had so much fun with *this* girl—and it's someone *else.*' "

In response, Mark-Paul merely shrugs. Isn't variety the spice of life?

Mark-Paul's idea of a dream date varies, depending on his mood and his companion's tastes. Instead of staging an elaborate evening, he likes to keep things spontaneous. "I do whatever comes to mind. That's more fun than actually planning something."

On an outing with Mark-Paul, you could end up anywhere. You might find yourself shaking hands with Mickey on Main Street at Disneyland. Or walking along the beach at Malibu to watch the sunset. Or shooting the Bigfoot Rapids at Knott's Berry Farm, an amusement park with a western theme.

Wherever he and his date decide to go, Mark-Paul likes to give her his personal attention. Double dates and dating in groups is out. "I've done that many times before, and it never works out," says Mark-Paul. "Especially with your best friend. You spend more time talking with your friend than with the girl."

In the past, Mark-Paul has dated actresses. At one point, he dated a few of the actresses with guest roles in "Saved by the Bell." "There were girls who would come on—guest stars—and I used to go out with some of them," Mark-Paul reveals.

But experience taught him that work and play do not mix well. He's decided that it's not wise to get involved with young actresses. "This is my work, and I can't do that," he says emphatically. For the time being, he's sworn off actresses and prefers to date girls who are not affected by Hollywood. He'd rather spend time with a girl who is "down-to-earth."

It's not easy for a guy like Mark-Paul to keep his love life a secret. With reporters asking questions and fans keeping an eye on him, he doesn't have a lot of privacy.

It's no help that his first kiss was witnessed by thousands of TV viewers who were watching "Good Morning, Miss Bliss". That's right, Mark-Paul Gosselaar had the first kiss of his life on-camera about three years ago. According to Mark-Paul, it was not the ideal way to kiss a girl. If you count the cast members and crew, there were dozens of people watching in the studio alone!

"He's talked about that in the teen magazines," Peter Engel says with a chuckle, "—how he just wanted to get it over with."

In the years he's worked on "Saved by the Bell," Mark-Paul has had to kiss on-camera dozens of times. Although he's a convincing actor, he assures you that it's just that— acting. His real romances do not take place on stage.

Since Kelly and Zack have long been an item on the show, Mark-Paul and costar Tiffani often land in each other's arms on the set. But off-camera, they're just good friends. When they traveled cross-country on a mall tour to promote the show, they became especially close.

Along with their parents and school-teacher Sidney Sharron, the popular two-some visited malls in cities like San Diego, Miami, and New York, to meet their fans and learn what kids across America had to say about "Saved by the Bell." Spending all that time on the road together made Mark-Paul and Tiffani friends for life.

Tiffani's mom explains, "When Tiffani and Mark-Paul went on tour together, I saw the two of them become very good friends, very close, almost like a brother-sister rela-tionship. Very protective. And that's good that they have that to share with one an-other."

Since Mark-Paul and Tiffani became pop-ular at the same time, they share many of the same demands, stresses, and pressures of Hollywood. Tiffani's mother adds: "I think they can handle the responsibility of being where they are and not letting it go to their heads. Otherwise, they'd beat up on each other," Robin finishes with an amused laugh.

Besides sealing his friendship with Tiffani, the mall tour brought one other thing into sharp focus for Mark-Paul. Somehow, after nearly ten years in show business, one season of playing Zack on "Saved by the Bell" had made him a celebrity.

Everywhere he went, whenever the announcer mentioned his name, girls and teens cheered and pushed toward him. Sidney Sharron, the gray-haired gentleman who teaches Mark-Paul on the set, was on tour with him. Sidney remembers the stir when one crowd got out of control.

"We came into a mall, and there were thousands of kids there. They had a security group, but the kids wanted to get closer," says Sidney. Mark-Paul was standing on a stage—a platform that had been erected in the mall. But it couldn't protect him from the crowd. "The crowd got closer," says Sidney, "and the platform started moving!"

The security team managed to keep the

crowd back, but suddenly dozens of girls were on Mark-Paul's trail. They found the van he was riding in. They followed him to the rest room. They even tried to chase him up the escalator!

Sidney remembers placing himself on the escalator between Mark-Paul and a determined group of fans. "I was like a guard between Mark-Paul and them. I mean, what can an old man do?" he teases. "At least I looked official. But I just laughed with them."

When Mark-Paul looks back on the mall experience, he gets thoughtful. Despite the eager mobs waiting for his autograph, despite the girls who have even asked him to sign their foreheads, he still doesn't see himself as famous.

"It's a rush when you hear the girls screaming," he says, "but the idea of fame hasn't really hit me yet. It's nice—but it's wild. In the back of my mind, I ask myself why? Because I don't see myself the way they see me."

In the back of *his* mind, Mark-Paul wonders if the hundreds of girls who write him dozens of fan letters are really in love with Zack Morris, adorable schemer and con artist—not Mark-Paul Gosselaar.

It's a tough call, but the distinction matters to Mark-Paul. For every one of Zack's pranks, Mark-Paul steels his will to follow the rules. For every word in one of Zack's brags, Mark-Paul just smiles, confident in the quiet truth. For every scheme that Zack dreams up, Mark-Paul puts solid, electric energy into action.

Zack is but a creation.

Mark-Paul Gosselaar is the real thing.

WATER FIGHTS AND ONSTAGE ANTICS: ON THE SET

It's Monday afternoon, and the cast and director of "Saved by the Bell" are blocking a scene from this week's show.

Since this episode is still in its early stages, everything's a little rough. And this scene's a tricky one. There are a dozen kids on the classroom set, and the director has to show them how to enter, move, and exit in a way that will look natural on-camera.

It's late in the day, and the actors are getting tired. Then suddenly Mark-Paul comes up with a burst of humor that recharges the cast.

The script calls for Mark-Paul to stand up, deliver a line, and exit with Mario. But instead of dragging through the scene, Mark-Paul leaps to his feet. With a sweeping gesture toward the door, he comes out with a line that's not in the script.

"To the batmobile, Robin!" he shouts to Mario, as he races to the door.

Mark-Paul's joke sends the cast and crew into a fit of laughter. But more importantly, it eases the tension and gives everyone the energy to finish the day's rehearsal.

Mark-Paul's generous spirit and contagious sense of fun propel him through every scene and make him a pleasure to watch on the set. And according to director Don Barnhart, Mark-Paul is a dream to direct.

"Doing a television series can make anyone tired," Don explains, "so it's important to keep everyone focused on positive levels. Since Mark-Paul is the driving force of 'Saved by the Bell,' I try to make sure he gets enough rest. And I try to keep negative distractions out of his way. I've found that if he gets tired, most likely the others will emotionally follow his lead. So it's important to help him balance his personal life, as well as his professional one."

As director, Don watches out for all of the cast members. But he pays special attention to Mark-Paul. "As a leader on the stage, Mark-Paul sets the tone for us. It's a responsibility not too many in this business relish, but I must say he handles it as a total professional," says Don.

That's not to say that Mark-Paul doesn't kid around with his costars. He still jokes with Mario, challenges Dustin, and arm wrestles with Tiffani.

In fact, when Tiffani's boyfriend, Eddie Garcia (from "The Guys Next Door"), was recently a guest on "Saved by the Bell," Mark-Paul tried to lure Eddie into mischief. But Eddie wouldn't bite. Mark-Paul was arm wrestling with Tiffani, and she was beginning to lose patience. When Tiffani started poking Mark-Paul in the elbow, he called out: "Eddie, help!"

Eddie glanced over and waved Mark-Paul off, as if to say, "You're on your own."

A key player in this hit show, Mark-Paul takes the responsibility, and the stress that goes with it, in stride. Despite an occasional incident, he tries to keep a low profile on the set.

But back in the early days of the program, when Mark-Paul was only fourteen years old, he and the other kids in the cast played mischievous games in the studio.

Sometimes, after rehearsals, Mark-Paul got into water fights with his costars and one crew member—a burly but gentle master carpenter the kids called Bobo.

Dustin Diamond, the rambunctious actor who plays Screech, recalls those zany games. Dustin and Mark-Paul usually teamed up against Bobo, who knew the set so well that he always managed to find a hiding place.

"Mark-Paul and I would chase him into alleys," says Dustin. "We'd be right behind Bobo; then he'd turn a corner and instantly he'd be gone. There were no doors, nothing to slip under, no way out!"

How did Bobo manage his disappearing

act? Dustin explains: "It turns out that he'd found some ropes and pulled himself up!"

Bobo smiles, then adds: "Then I'd get behind you and squirt you."

When it came to water fights, the kids used everything from plastic bottles of mineral water to full-fledged water pistols. "We've got water guns that are supersoakers," Dustin explains. "You just keep pulling the trigger."

Television studios are actually enormous buildings—sometimes the size of an airport hangar. Besides the sets you see on TV—the three-walled rooms built to resemble a classroom or the Max—there are dozens of nooks and crannies behind the scenes. Lofts, ladders, catwalks, and huge storage spaces surround the onstage area.

And the cast couldn't resist exploring that unchartered territory. "Mark-Paul and I have been through every crevice on this sound stage," Dustin insists.

Once, the man in charge of special effects helped Mark-Paul play a trick on Tiffani. The two guys set up some spooky effects in a prop storage room. They took a life-size poster of Tiff that had been used in an earlier show and focused some special lights on it. With the bait set, they put their plan into motion.

Now sitting together on the set, the actors listen intently as Tiffani recalls how Mark-Paul lured her into the room. "Mark-Paul said, 'Come here. I have to show you something.' "

Curious, she followed him over to the prop room. "I open the door," says Tiffani. "It's pitch-black in there. Then the lights are flickering. I turn around and I see a poster of me and I scream: 'Ahhh!' "

The cast members howl with laughter. Mark-Paul, one of the pranksters behind this scheme, sits smiling in the corner, his arms folded. In all the tales of backstage antics, Mark-Paul has a starring role.

Once, when Mark-Paul and Dustin were exploring the studio, they were almost caught and taken to task for their mischief.

They had climbed a ladder to a catwalk that runs over the stage. Since there were no lights on the catwalk, Mark-Paul and Dustin paused, squinting into the darkness. Mark-Paul volunteered to go first. He crawled along the catwalk until he came to a door.

"Hey, Dustin, check it out," Mark-Paul whispered as he opened the door. To his surprise, there was a woman on the other side! The door led to one of the studio offices.

Dustin recalls: "I heard this lady say, 'Excuse me, may I help you, young man?' "

Mark-Paul winces when he thinks of the close call. "I said, 'Oh, no, I'll see you later.' " Then he closed the door and ran.

Quick and athletic, Mark-Paul had a reputation for beating hasty retreats when backstage antics backfired. On one occasion, when Mark-Paul, Dustin, and Tiffani were exploring the studio, Mark-Paul made such a quick getaway that Dustin was stranded behind.

They were exploring a dark corridor between walls of some sets. Tiffani explains: "It's pitch-dark in there because it's between the walls. And the area is filled with a lot of wood and cross beams."

The teens were able to explore in the light coming from the open door. But they decided to make a quick getaway when they heard the scratching and scurrying of mice!

Mark-Paul darted out the door. Tiffani followed on his heels. But when the door slammed shut by accident, there wasn't enough light for Dustin to find his way out!

Dustin remembers sitting in the dark, calling: "Guys, please, let me out of here! Guys—this is not funny!"

Now that it's all over, Dustin sees the humor in the episode. In fact, all of the cast members fondly look back on their early adventures. But the days of backstage antics are over. These kids have turned into attractive teenagers before our eyes.

"These kids really have grown up," says executive producer Peter Engel. "Mark-Paul used to come up to here on me," Engel says, holding his hand to his chin. "He's gone from fourteen to seventeen. And he picked me up the other day and carried me off the set!"

As the kids have grown up, they've also

learned to express themselves—on-camera, and behind the scenes.

"When we get together, all the kids hug each other and the other adults," Peter explains. "At the beginning, Mark-Paul never could hug anyone. Now he's the biggest hugger of all."

Don Barnhart considers Mark-Paul's growth to be an asset to the show. "I love Mark-Paul," says Don. "It's been exciting to see his growth as an actor and as a good human being. I'm proud of him and his work. He makes it a pleasure to step onto a stage."

With his steely discipline and surprising sense of humor, Mark-Paul makes acting a pleasure for his costars, too. And sometimes, his bursts of wit make it onto the air.

That was the case in a recent episode. In one of the fantasy segments, Mark-Paul and Elizabeth Berkley, the actress who plays Jessie, were dressed up as old women. Decked out in a wig, dress, nylons, and high heels, Mark-Paul—or rather, Zack—was spying on Slater and Kelly.

When Mark-Paul and Elizabeth jumped up and tried to exit, Elizabeth made it off-stage. But Mark-Paul's exit wasn't so graceful.

As the director put it: "Mark-Paul slipped—wham! He did a three-pointer right on the deck. And of course, it was hysterical. He got up. He didn't hurt himself, so we just kept it in because it worked so well."

After the producers decided to incorporate the "fall" into the show, Mark-Paul polished it up even more. "At one point," says Don, "he got up and curtsied! And that made it to the air."

Spontaneous creativity—that's what makes Mark-Paul different from hundreds of other actors who just read their lines.

One day during rehearsal on the set, Mark-Paul gave a scene a new twist that made the cast and crew members double over with laughter.

In the script, Kelly was at a party with her new boyfriend, a rock star who had a few bad habits. Mark-Paul was supposed to enter the room, say "Come on, Kelly," and exit with her.

In a way, Zack is helping Kelly escape from the apartment. So Mark-Paul took the scene a step further. Instead of entering through the door, Mark-Paul ran behind the set and called to the director, "Wait—how about this?"

With that, he leaped through the open window of the apartment on the set. Placing his hands on his hips in Superman-style, he said in a deep voice, "Come on, Kelly." Then Mark-Paul crossed to the sofa, picked Tiffani up in his arms, and carried her out of the room!

The crew roared with laughter. Appreciating Mark-Paul's spark of creativity, the director let everyone take a minute to have some fun.

The actors returned to their positions to try the scene again. This time, Mark-Paul leaped through the window and sang the Mighty Mouse theme song: "Here I come to save the day. . ."

Once again, the cast and crew were delighted. The other teen actors began to sing the cartoon theme, which would become their inside joke of the week.

With an amused smile, the director shrugged and quipped, "I suppose it's all in the reading of the lines."

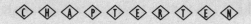

AN
ICY
HEAVEN

The notion of fame is so far from Mark-Paul Gosselaar's mind that he's still surprised when people recognize him in public places.

He was recently walking through a shopping mall near his home when a boy stopped him and asked: "Are you Zack?"

"I had to think about it for a minute before I said yes," Mark-Paul recalls. "It just didn't register that I was Zack—"

Mark-Paul hasn't come to terms with the idea that he is, by Hollywood standards, a star.

"Lots of teens ask, 'Hey, how does it feel

to be a star?' " he explains. "First of all, I hate the word *star*. And how do you tell them that it's not what they think it is?"

The glitter and glitz of Hollywood have not impressed Mark-Paul. "I hate Hollywood's this and that . . . it's not so much the demands. There's so much energy wasted. The way people dress, the way they present themselves as if they're trying to impress people." In his baseball cap and comfortably worn sweatshirt, he waves off the activity on the rest of the set. "I could really care less."

In a way, the reality of fame and fans and show business has taken Mark-Paul Gosselaar by surprise.

"I didn't think show business was anything like this," he says. "I saw it as an icy heaven . . . something far away. I didn't know how things were done. If I knew back then what I know now, I would have said, 'Let's think about this for a minute.' "

A serious expression comes over his face as he tries to scrutinize the past. A moment later, he grins and tosses back his blond head of hair. "On the other hand, I'm glad I got this part."

For Mark-Paul, it's hard to imagine his teen years without the fun-loving schemes of Zack Morris on "Saved by the Bell." But the role did not come without some sacrifices.

To put 100 percent of his energy into the role of Zack, Mark-Paul had to give up his high-school years and his free time. According to Mark-Paul, those were the two biggest sacrifices: "Your social life and school. I had to give up high school. I only spent a few months in a regular high school. The rest of the time I've been tutored."

Although Mark-Paul started ninth grade in a conventional school, after a few months, he had to withdraw and enroll at the Learning Post, a special school for actors. He would have liked to stay in his old school, but, as Mark-Paul puts it: "Sometimes things just don't work out."

Now you're probably saying: *Give up school? No problem!*

But imagine your life without all the *events* of high school: pep rallies, class elections, field trips, choir concerts, club meetings, car washes, football games, and proms. Wouldn't you feel as if you missed something?

More than anything, Mark-Paul misses the sports teams and events of a real high school. "When I was ten, I used to be a really good runner," he says. "I played some flag football and baseball. But that's probably all I know about school."

When Mark-Paul attended school, he kept a low profile. No one in his class knew that he was doing commercials or going on auditions for TV shows.

"I wasn't really known at school," he says. "I was quiet. Some people wondered 'Who is this guy?' because I was always coming in and out. I didn't want to tell them I was an actor. But then when I did this show, everyone went 'Ooohhh.' "

Perhaps the most difficult choice came when he realized he would never be able to participate in high-school football. "Suddenly I realized, 'Well, now you can't play football.' " At the age of fourteen, Mark-Paul had to choose between playing the sports he loved and acting out the role of Zack Morris.

Tough choice.

Fortunately for TV viewers and fans, Mark-Paul decided to stick with the "Saved by the Bell" gang.

And for all the sacrifices, Mark-Paul is the first to point out the advantages of his TV role. He is well paid. He has made on-screen friends with kids across America. And he's doing something he loves.

"The money is a plus," Mark-Paul admits. "Because of this show, I'll get to go to college. And you get to meet people. Some of them are really great."

And though he tries to avoid the trappings of stardom, Mark-Paul has been deeply touched by his fans around the world. He was especially moved at the deluge of mail that came in after he was injured in 1990.

While rehearsing for a trapeze stunt in the "Circus of the Stars" TV event, Mark-Paul took a bad fall on the net and broke his breastbone. Although Mark-Paul's injury was not serious, he couldn't work until the broken bone healed.

The cast and crew of "Saved by the Bell"

had to delay production of the show for three weeks while Mark-Paul recovered.

When worried fans began asking questions, the producers decided to run a quick message. In a thirty-second spot, they announced that Mark-Paul was fine and recovering quickly. Then a special address flashed on the screen, showing fans where they could write to Mark-Paul if they wanted to reach him directly.

The address was only on the screen for a few seconds. But the response to the message bowled over the show's producers—and Mark-Paul himself.

Get-well cards and letters for Mark-Paul flooded in. As producer Franco Bario recalls, "He got thousands and thousands of pieces of mail right away—within days."

Some of the mail came from very young kids. "Three-year-olds," says Mark-Paul's mother. "You could see it in the handwriting—crayon on tiny scraps of paper." There were also cards and letters from older viewers, male and female, teens and "tweens"—kids between the ages of nine and twelve.

The viewer response was nothing short of amazing. Although Mark-Paul was less than thrilled to be laid up with a broken bone, he appreciated the outpouring of good wishes.

Besides having supportive fans, Mark-Paul finds other benefits in his acting career. He enjoys the art of acting itself—especially in front of a live audience. One of his favorite parts of working on "Saved by the Bell" is escaping into the role of Zack Morris.

"You get to play roles that you never play in real life," says Mark-Paul. "It's sort of an escape from reality. It's not you, it's somebody else. You can forget about things when you're doing it."

When he goes on-camera, Mark-Paul manages to leave the stress and pressure behind. "When they say 'five . . . four . . . three . . . two . . . ,' it really doesn't matter what happened before you went on. Before you go on, you might have so much on your shoulders. But when you're acting, the pressure's gone."

He stares off into the distance and adds: "Acting is almost like a drug. If people could act . . . " His voice trails off, and he shakes his head. Nix that thought. Acting may be the perfect escape for Mark-Paul Gosselaar, but it probably wouldn't work for everyone.

For now, Mark-Paul Gosselaar's future in front of the camera seems like a sure thing. He recently went on an audition for a TV movie, and the casting director recognized him from "Saved by the Bell."

"Now they usually know who I am," he says with a pleased grin. "I forgot my résumé, and she already knew what I did."

In a profession that's tough to break into, Mark-Paul now has a definite advantage. "It's not like it used to be when I was pounding down doors," he agrees.

Mark-Paul has also considered alternatives to an acting career. He knows that many child stars have grown up and out of the profession.

If Mark-Paul's TV and film roles should start to dwindle, he won't be devastated. He is determined to try other professions. "If it doesn't work out, then I'm going on to other things," says Mark-Paul. "But if it does work out, then that's fine, too."

What would he do if his acting career should end?

"I'm definitely going to college," he says. He's also interested in pursuing law or "any kind of professional sports." That fiery torch for football is still burning in the heart of this athletic guy.

Otherwise, Mark-Paul Gosselaar is open to a wide variety of career possibilities—although this seventeen-year-old hunk doesn't want to make any final choices in the near future. This is a guy chock-full of creative energy. A casual guy who likes to keep things spontaneous and spur-of-the-moment.

So far, that philosophy has worked well for Mark-Paul Gosselaar, Saturday's star.

AT A GLANCE...
MARK-PAUL GOSSELAAR

HAIR:	Blond
EYES:	Hazel
BIRTHDAY:	March 1, 1974
BIRTHPLACE:	Panorama City, CA
ASTROLOGICAL SIGN:	Pisces
HEIGHT:	5'10"
WEIGHT:	165 pounds
PARENTS:	Paula and Hans
SIBLINGS:	Mike, Sylvia, Linda, all older
HOBBIES:	All sports—especially football and bicycle motorcross racing

EXPERIENCE:

● —Plays the lovable, infamous Zack Morris on "Saved by the Bell"

● —Played the same role on the Disney channel's "Good Morning, Miss Bliss"

● —Guest appearances on "Charles in Charge" and "Murphy Brown"

● —Starred in PBS television movie *Necessary Parties*

THESE ARE A FEW OF HIS FAVORITE THINGS

Have you been wondering how to get to Mark-Paul Gosselaar's heart? Here are a few of his all-time favorite things. . . .

FAVORITE COLORS:	red, black, and white
FAVORITE SCHOOL SUBJECT:	lunch period!
FAVORITE MOVIE:	*The Silence of the Lambs*
FAVORITE SPORTS:	football and motorcross

FAVORITE BOOK:	*The Heart Is a Lonely Hunter*
FAVORITE FOOD:	Everything—as long as it doesn't bite back! (We know he loves Japanese food and Thai iced tea.)
FAVORITE HOBBY:	weight lifting
FAVORITE DREAM CAR:	Porsche 911
FAVORITE ACTOR:	Alan Arkin
FAVORITE ACTRESS:	none (The position is open, ladies!)
FAVORITE TV SHOW:	"In Living Color"

FAVORITE
VACATION SPOT: Fiji Islands
FAVORITE QUALITIES
IN A FRIEND: honesty and
humor

WAIT A MINUTE, MISTER POSTMAN!

If you would like to write to Mark-Paul Gosselaar, you can contact him at these addresses:

Mark-Paul Gosselaar Fan Club
P.O. Box 801024
Santa Clarita, CA 91380-1024

or

Mark-Paul Gosselaar
c/o "Saved by the Bell"
NBC-TV
3000 West Alameda Blvd.
Burbank, CA 91523

QUIZ

How well do you know Mark-Paul Gosselaar? Here's a chance to test yourself on the real story behind those sparkling hazel eyes and that mischievous smile.

1. Where are Mark-Paul's parents from?

a. Iceland

b. Kalamazoo

c. Holland

d. Bayside

2. How did Mark-Paul get his start in show business?

a. He won a talent search contest.

b. He and his friends put on shows in the garage.

c. He starred in a school play.

d. He signed up at an agency and started modeling.

3. What musical inspired Mark-Paul to pursue acting?

a. *Annie*

b. *Phantom of the Opera*

c. *The Sound of Music*

d. *Grease*

4. What tricky task did Mark-Paul have to do in a cookie commercial?

a. bake a batch of cookies

b. juggle cookies

c. catch a cookie in his mouth

d. dress up as a giant cookie

5. How long does it take to rehearse and tape one episode of "Saved by the Bell?"

a. thirty minutes

b. five days

c. six weeks

d. one year

6. Mark-Paul would love to attend a real school. What does he miss most?

a. school sports—like football

b. detention

c. running for class president

d. auto shop

7. What do Mark-Paul and his brother, Mike, do together?

a. play chess

b. mow the lawn

c. repair dirt bikes

d. groom horses

8. What is Mark-Paul's idea of a dream date?

a. dinner at a restaurant on the beach

b. a trip to Disneyland

c. splashing through the Bigfoot Rapids at Knott's Berry Farm

d. Any of the above—whatever you're both in the mood for

9. What happened when Mark-Paul was rehearsing for "Circus of the Stars"?

a. He was scratched by a tiger.

b. He fell on the net and broke his breastbone.

c. He fed peanuts to the elephants.

d. He stubbed his toe on the center ring.

10. Where would Mark-Paul like to go for a dream vacation?

a. pearl diving in Japan

b. body boarding in the Fiji Islands

c. yodeling in Switzerland

d. Whale watching in Nova Scotia

11. What type of home do Mark-Paul and his family live in?

a. a three-bedroom house in the suburbs of L.A.

b. a penthouse in Beverly Hills

c. a beach house in Malibu

d. a restored castle in Scotland

12. What role does Mark-Paul play on "Saved by the Bell"?

a. Screech, the lovable but nerdy inventor

b. Slater, the streetwise, cool kid

c. Mr. Belding, the concerned principal

d. Zack Morris, the adorable schemer

ANSWER KEY:

1-C	7-C
2-D	8-D
3-A	9-B
4-C	10-B
5-B	11-A
6-A	12-D

How did you rate? Check your amount of correct answers to see how well you know Mark-Paul.

CORRECT ANSWERS

1: You need to be "Saved by the Bell"!

2: Please report to Mr. Belding's office—pronto!

3: Say it isn't so!

4: Mark-Paul isn't your man—but Screech may be!

5: Mark-Paul isn't for you. How about Mario?

6: Not bad. Try again.

7: Time to join Mark-Paul's fan club.

8: Awesome!

9: Welcome to Bayside High!

10: Way to go, girl!

11: Aw, come on. You must have met Mark-Paul!

12: You did it! Mark-Paul will pick you up at seven.